The Importance of Waiting

By: LaToya Sneed

BK
ROYSTON
Publishing

BK Royston Publishing
P. O. Box 4321
Jeffersonville, IN 47131
502-802-5385
http://www.bkroystonpublishing.com
bkroystonpublishing@gmail.com

© Copyright – 2021

All Rights Reserved. No part of this book may be reproduced, stored in a retrieval system, or transmitted by any means without the written permission of the author.

Cover Design: Elite Cover Designs

ISBN-13: 978-1-951941-86-4

King James Version Scriptural Text – Public Domain
New International Version (NIV) - Holy Bible, New International Version®, NIV® Copyright ©1973, 1978, 1984, 2011 by Biblica, Inc.® Used by permission. All rights reserved worldwide.

Printed in the United States of America

Dedication

All the young teens around the world! I encourage you to keep this verse hidden in your heart as you go through life facing all kinds of temptations and choices.

Proverbs 3:5&6 (NIV) - "Trust in the Lord with all your heart and lean not to your own understanding, but in all your ways submit to Him and He will make your paths straight."

Table of Contents

Dedication	iii
Introduction	vii
Leader	1
Relationships With the Opposite Sex	9
The Ultimate Relationship	21
The Word While You Wait	35
About the Author	61

Introduction

I am very worried and concerned about this generation and the others to follow. Their minds have been warped with so much deceit of this world that they do not realize the very things that are destroying them. This world is teaching our young babies and youth to not place any value on their lives and to just live any way that they please. Do all you can they say, you are young and you only live once. That is about the only Truth that I do agree with and that you do live only once, but what a shame to go through life living any kind of way you please and to lose your soul at the end. In the Bible it states in the book of Mark, chapter 8, verse 36, "what does it profit a man (woman) to gain the whole world yet forfeit (lose) his (her) soul?" (ESV) I know you say, "Here she goes with that Bible stuff. No one has time for that." Let me inform you that if you hang tight with me, you might just learn a new way of living that is actually for your good and those around you. This short book has been put together to encourage or challenge you to view your life from a different perspective. A perspective that is set in place not to harm you but guide you to a life that is full of Freedom, Love (unconditional), Grace and Mercy.

You ask, "what is Grace and Mercy?" I am so glad you asked. Grace in simple terms can be defined as "getting what you do not deserve." For example, God sending his Son Jesus to die on the cross to save all of humanity, even those who would not believe. At times when we sin willingly, he still provides for us, loves us unconditionally, and we can never pay Him back for giving up his own life on that cross. Talk about a Good God!! I don't know about you, but if you were to wrong someone today, they would not be so forgiving as God; they would be ready to seek revenge, but no, not our God, He is eagerly waiting for you to turn back to Him! On the flip side you have Mercy, which is withholding punishment that is due to you. For example, when we commit a sin against God he has every right to take us out. Why? Because he is that powerful. Instead he allows Mercy and does not give us the punishment due to us, but He allows us chance after chance to get it right with Him. Now please keep in mind that does not mean that we should continue to do wrong because we know he will forgive. Just like a parent gets tired when you keep on disobeying and gives you consequences, so does our Father in heaven, we are not to take him for granted! I hope that with the explanations given above it has provided you with a better appreciation and understanding of Grace and Mercy and how thankful we should be to know we have access to a GOD who wants nothing but the best for His children!

LEADER

Being a leader in today's society is not always the most popular thing to do. You will sometimes have to deal with some of the negative feedback from your peers because you don't always do what the (in-crowd) is doing. Sometimes people will pick on you for standing up for what you believe, all because they do not understand you as an individual. There are a lot different scenarios that could play out when you have the inner desire to do the right thing. Whatever the case may be, I want to personally encourage you to stay the course of being a positive role model or leader. You never know who is out there watching you and admiring your braveness; your positive life example could be the very thing to allow another person the courage to become positive as well. In the Bible it speaks of being a light, in Matthew 5:16: "Let your light shine before men that they may see your good works and glorify your Father in Heaven." (NKJV) So you see, being a leader in life is not meant to cause you harm, shame or feel like an outcast in this world, but it is meant for you to be set apart, and that, my friend, is being the light that was mentioned in the verse.

Let me share a little of my childhood with you. Growing up as a young girl and being raised by my grandparents I was not allowed to participate in a lot of things as other kids my age. There were times that I felt like my peers were able to enjoy all the fun things in life and I was missing out. It was later in life that I understood that my grandmother (God rest her soul) did not allow me to participate in some things, because she was trying to protect me from having to experience a whole lot of unnecessary heartaches and set-backs as much as possible. I sit and think back on it now as an adult and further realize that she was doing it all for my own good. Who knows, if she had allowed me to go to those parties, ride with those friends, go that club, where I would be at right now? I could very easily have been strung out on drugs or sleeping with anybody to fill empty voids in my life. I would have been living life in circles not going anywhere but right back to the chaotic mess I would have created.

So I share that with you to remember that being a leader is not a bad thing and don't let anyone tell you differently. It shows that you have a mind of your own and you are not afraid to use it. It allows others to see that you are not that easily influenced by the negative things that they have to offer to throw your life off track. I want you to reflect on your life and take the time to answer the two questions on the next page. Remember — this is your book to keep and look back over, so you answer them how you feel, all I ask is that you be honest with yourself:

Do I consider myself more of a follower or leader and why?

_____
_____
_____
_____
_____
_____
_____
_____
_____
_____
_____
_____
_____
_____
_____
_____
_____
_____
_____
_____
_____
_____
_____

Based on my answer above, what can I do to better myself or those around me?

_____
_____
_____
_____
_____
_____
_____
_____
_____
_____
_____
_____
_____
_____
_____
_____
_____
_____
_____
_____
_____
_____

It is more important to wait and take your time to enjoy life in the most positive way possible, than to feel like you have to rush and experience everything right now. Rushing through life will only lead you to make impulse decisions, which in return will lead you down a path of regrets and disappointments. Our ultimate goal in life is to please God, and the only way to do that is ask Him daily to guide our steps, take him at his word and then follow (refer back to Proverbs 3:5&6!)

Relationships (With the Opposite Sex)

Oh my! The Hot topic, relationships, it seems that every young person wants to say that they have a boyfriend/girlfriend (or bae as they call it today). This topic here can get you caught up in so many emotions that you as a young teenager are not mature enough to fully handle just yet. Trust me, if we as adults are still learning, there is no way that young men and woman as yourselves have all the answers. The purpose of this section of the book is to encourage you to understand the importance of waiting before taking your relationships to the level of sexual intimacy.

I know all too well from firsthand experience of regretting and wishing I had waited until marriage before making this decision. Some people reading this are thinking, "Is she serious that is not the way things are today? Everybody is doing it!" I want to take you down a little journey of my own personal experience in this area and the chaos that came from making this one unwise decision. Maybe you will take heed and learn from it and maybe you won't, but it is still my responsibility to share with you in hope that someone will listen. Remember, I too was once your age and thought some of the same ways you do.

All throughout my middle school and high school years I was more of the outcast and didn't have a boyfriend. However, those around me were more experienced because I could hear some of the conversations about things that they had done with others. So when I did meet a guy and made the choice to take the relationship to the next level, I can honestly say that I had regrets. I pray that some young lady or man reading this would Truly learn from my mistakes. I hope you realize the real importance of waiting and being that leader rather than a follower as mentioned earlier in the book. So many rewards come to the ones who wait, but so much unnecessary destruction comes to those who are so quick to do things your own way.

I was in my junior year in high school (April 2001) and I was introduced to my first boyfriend. Now you know that your first boyfriend/girlfriend you are just head over heels for. I mean you will do anything for that person to make them happy and you always wanted to spend time together; it's like the two of you are inseparable. One thing I knew for sure was that I was not going to have sex with this boy because my grandmother had put the fear of God in me when it came to that area, but boy did that change. I must say I gave in for reasons that were not good enough and in return caused me to have even further regrets. I had thoughts in my head that if I continued to push him away then he would find someone else or just leave me alone. My final thought that I allowed myself to go through with it this particular time, is that this was the way for me to show him that I really loved him. BIG MISTAKE, in so many ways!! I have now given up a part of myself that I could never get back for a reason that was foolish. After that moment, I remember feeling a sense of uncertainty within myself and thinking what did I just do. Nonetheless, I continued this cycle for many years to come, I figured once I did it I could not stop now. What would he think of me if I said, "oh I can't do this anymore"? I was such a people pleaser at this point of my life that I did whatever to please the next person and just hid my feelings. I was in the vicious cycle for 13 years. Yes, you read that correctly: 13 years of a bunch of chaos all because of one foolish mistake and not knowing how to escape. We lived together during this time, of course, and along the way we had four baby boys together. My boys were the only blessing out of my mess that I can say I am thankful to God for, but the sad part is they grew up in a household that was not healthy by any means. Side bar, it is very important that every choice we make in life, good/bad, never affects only you but it affects those around you.

In this case, it affected my boys tremendously as well me; they had to witness their mother being abused mentally and physically and fall into a depression. So many days I just wanted to be alone so I would close my door and just stay in there all day, except to come out and feed them. Although their father and I lived together, his mindset was to be out in the streets, so he was hardly ever home. So, I guess you can say in a sense I was just as less of a mother to them there as he was a father to them away. There was a lot on my plate while we were together. I had to make sure I maintained a job because all the responsibilities fell on me to provide for our family, and it was draining! One positive thing I did do for my boys was get them involved in sports. They played T-ball and football. I did enjoy going to their games and cheering them on: they brought some joy to my heart to see them happy doing something they loved. You may be wondering all this can happen from making one bad mistake. Why yes it can, and when you don't correct the problem and you allow it to continue, nothing good will come of it until you decide to make a change.

When you decide to make the decision to have sex with someone that is not your husband/wife and you go against God's plan, it contaminates your mind. It makes you connect with that individual on such a deeper level than you understand. It distorts the mind and you will start to notice that you think and do things that are out of the ordinary for you. This is because this act is a transfer of spirits between you, the individual you are sleeping with, and whoever else either of you may have slept with prior. This is because your bodies have become one flesh. If the individual you have chosen to sleep with is not a person of good character and desires things of this world, but that is not the path of your choice, you have now entered into a world of chaos. In I Corinthians 6:18–20 it speaks of fleeing of sexual immortality. The scripture says the following: "Flee from sexual immorality. All other sins a person commits are outside of the body, but whoever sins sexually, sins against their own body. Do you not know that your bodies are temples of the Holy Spirit, who is in you, whom you have received from God? You are not your own; you were bought at a price. Therefore, honor God with your bodies." (NIV)

I have to live with the fact that I gave up my body to its own lustful desires and for the pleasure of others. As I grow older and wiser, I realize what the verses mentioned above mean, that my body is not my own and I am to be intentional to honor God. It took me some years after the relationship to get this point in my life but my prayer is for you reading this book to grasp this concept way sooner. Once you understand this, you start to look at choices you make in life differently and will realize the importance of waiting!

Waiting not just when it comes to giving up your body but waiting when it comes to making any decisions in your life. You want to be sure that you seek God's guidance first. Isaiah 55:8 say this: "For my thoughts are not your thoughts, neither are your ways my ways, declares the Lord." (NIV) So what better person to help guide us in life than the one who created this world and us!

The Ultimate Relationship

This book would not be complete if I did not offer to some and remind others of the ultimate relationship to have with the one and only, who came to this world to offer salvation to us all, Jesus Christ. Although some will not accept this precious relationship, don't let that be you. Don't be the one to miss out on the best gift that will only add value and true meaning to your life. As it states in Jeremiah 29:11–12, "'For I know the plans I have for you,' declares the Lord, 'plans to give you hope and a future. Then you will call on me and come and pray to me, and I will listen to you.'" As you think back to some of the things that were mentioned in this book, use the lines on the next page to write down some things that you would like to do differently to better enhance your life and the lives of those around you. If you remember, we mentioned earlier that every choice in life not only affects you but also those around you. One thing I was taught is if you write things down, you are 10 times more likely to do it!

Changes I need to make in my life:

_____
_____
_____
_____
_____
_____
_____
_____
_____
_____
_____
_____
_____
_____
_____
_____
_____
_____
_____
_____
_____
_____
_____
_____

As you continue your journey in this life, I can promise you that you will go through some things good and bad. One thing to realize is that when you decide to give your life over to Christ and the trials come, you have a savior who will be there with you along the way. Our trials come to test our Faith, to build character and to share a testimony with others of how good God is and how our Faith in Him brought us through. There will be people to tell you how unpopular this life is with Christ and how it is boring. Oh my dear friend, it is quite the opposite. When you take time to read about Jesus' life and learn of His ways, you will better understand how much more peaceful and better your life is. As you spend time daily communicating with HIM and listening for Him to speak back to you, the more purposeful your life will seem. God's Word is here to teach us how we should live, how we should appear set apart from others who aren't following Him, not set apart to appear better than others but set apart in a sense that others will look at you and notice something different or peculiar. This is what leads to an opportunity to testify or share with others about our God and how marvelous He is.

God is a God of love and forgiveness! So no matter what you may have done up until this point in your life or may feel ashamed of or even feel unworthy. I am here to remind you that there is nothing in life that can make Him love any less. All he asks is that you accept Him into your life, surrender, allow Him to lead you, and you, too, shall be saved. You don't have to be in a church setting or any specific place to accept Him; this can be done right now where you are. Repeat the following verses in Romans 10:9&10, "If you declare with your mouth Jesus is Lord, and believe in your heart that God raised Jesus from the dead, you will be saved. For it is with the Heart that you believe and are justified, and it is with your mouth that you profess your faith and are saved." (NIV) Once you have read those verses for yourself and mean it, then, my dear friend, you are saved and adopted in the kingdom of Christ. At this instant you receive the Holy Spirit within you. It is placed to guide you in this life's journey if you allow it. When you find yourself slipping back to some old habits or things that are not of Christ, remember to ask for forgiveness, repent and forgive yourself. That way you can continue on through life not dwelling on your mistakes you have made, but so that you can be the very best "you" moving forward. I highly encourage you to get connected with a local church that you feel God has led you to so that you can be a disciple and connected with other believers. This journey can be difficult at times, because the flesh will always be at war with the ways of Christ, and you will want to seek help from people who are traveling the same path as you. I can guarantee you that no matter what you face this life with Christ will be a very REWARDING one!!

To those of you readers that have accepted Christ but have fallen back to your old way of living, let me remind you that we serve a God that is full of Grace (give us what is not deserved — salvation) and Mercy (withholds punishment that is deserved). Refer to Ephesians 2:4-5, "But because of his great love for us, God, who is rich in mercy, made us alive with Christ even when we were dead in transgressions—it is by grace you have been saved." (NIV) So you must know that God is waiting with open arms for you to return back to Him, but it is up to you to make that choice: just know that His love is unconditional! A good reference regarding an example of unconditional love is the story of the prodigal son located in the book of Luke15:11–32, which I recommend to read for yourself when you have time. To paraphrase the story, it is about a father who had two sons, and his younger son decided he wanted his inheritance now (basically so he could go out and have a good time). So his father gave him what he asked for and he went on about his way; he went through his money so fast on unnecessary things that he was down to nothing and could not even eat. He was so poor because of the unwise decisions that he went to work with the pigs in hopes to get some of their food and could not. When he finally came to his senses, he started to realize that this was not the life for him and that he had sinned against his father. 'I must return and ask my father for forgiveness," he thought. Sure enough, when he returned, his father saw him coming. He was so happy, he welcomed his son home and forgave him. The father got everyone together and celebrated the return of his lost son with a big feast. However, the brother who had stayed behind was not at all happy. He could not understand that all the pain that his brother had put his father through by leaving and then returns with celebration. However, the father had to remind the brother what this celebration really means. The celebration was that the son was dead but now alive again!! Wow, what an interesting story of unconditional love. My friend, this is the same unconditional love our Father in heaven has for us when we go astray. He welcomes us back as if we have not done any wrong.

As I bring this book to a close always remember the importance of waiting for God's direction to lead and guide you to make the best decisions in life. When you choose to do things your way, be ready for the consequences that come with it. God is a loving God but He allows you to make a choice, and if you choose opposite from Him, He will have to discipline you, just like a parent who corrects or disciplines their child, but He will never leave you. He is always waiting for your return back to Him and to give you chances to try again. I love you and hope this book has encouraged you to lean on God for everything. Be Blessed!!!!!!

Reflection

The Word While You Wait

1. Anxiety:

1 Peter 5:7 (NIV) -Cast all your anxiety on him because he cares for you.

**When you are feeling nervous, worried or not at peace about any decision in life. Always remember that God is waiting for you to talk to Him first! He wants to calm your spirit so you can hear clearly from Him to make the next move in your life. Trust me His way is always the best way with the best results! **

Prayer: Lord God, whenever I feel an uneasy spirit within me about any decision in my life, give me the strength to give it over to You. I know that You love me and You want nothing but the best for me.

2. **Character:**

I Corinthians 15:33 (NIV) -Do not be misled: "Bad Company corrupts good character."

**It is important to be aware of the company we hang around. We want to be sure that our life represents who we say we are and not allow others to dictate ours. We want to be the light no matter what situation we may find ourselves in. **

Prayer: Dear Lord, I pray that I can be the best version of you daily no matter what may come my way. When I fail, help me to make it right.

3. **Comparison**:

Galatians 6:4 (NIV) -Each one should test their own actions. Then they can take pride in themselves alone, without comparing themselves to someone else.

**Simply means not comparing yourself to someone else's success or accomplishments. Get up and do the work yourself, then you, too, can be proud of yourself. As the saying goes, "you never know a person's struggle to get to where they are in life." We all have different paths set out for us in life; you just have to seek out yours. **

Prayer: Lord God on this day, show me my path you have set out for my life so that I may be accomplished in you and not in myself.

4. **Depression:**

Psalms 34:18 (NIV) -The Lord is close to the brokenhearted and saves those who are crushed in spirit.

**Depression can take you to a dark and scary place. Please know that God does not like to see His children hurting. This is the time to get real and personal with God and cry out to Him. Share your feelings, your hurts and watch Him turn your sadness to Joy, but only when you release it to Him. **

Prayer: Father God when I fall into these dark places in my life and I am all alone, please hear my cry; fill my empty void and allow me peace. I give my unhealthy thoughts over to You because I can't handle them and exchange them for Your love!

5. **Anger:**
James 1:19-20 (NIV) -My dear brother and sisters, take note of this: Everyone should be quick to listen, slow to speak and slow to become angry, because human anger does not produce the righteousness that God desires.

**We were given three simple steps: Quick to listen, slow to speak, and slow to anger. I believe these were set in place to allow us time to think before we respond to any situations we encounter. It is wise advice to follow so we don't say hurtful things that we cannot take back, because words can hurt deeper than actions. **

Prayer: Lord, when I am angry, I ask for Your Holy Spirit to control my thoughts and my speech so that I may respond reflecting You and not my flesh. If I have angered someone, help me to be humble and make the situation right.

6. Contentment:

Philippians 4:12 (NIV) -I know what it is to be in need, and I know what it is to have plenty. I have learned the secret of being content in any and every situation, whether well fed or hungry, whether living in plenty or in want.

We are to realize that whatever your status may be in life, rather rich or poor that God is still providing. We have to be okay with our current situation and trust that He will bring us through. Even when it looks impossible still believe! Be sure to Thank God for what you have, because greed can cause Him to take it away very quickly, so stay humble.

Prayer: Father God, I pray that no matter what my surrounding circumstances may be in life, I will learn to be content, because I know that you are in control.

7. **Discipleship:**

Luke 9:23-24 (ESV) And he said to all, "If anyone would come after me, let him deny himself and take up his cross daily and follow me. For whoever would save his life will lose it, but whoever loses his life for my sake will save it."

Denying yourself means to ask God daily to remove anything in you that does not please Him so that He can fully use you. Losing your life does not mean literally, it means that you now live for Christ and no longer for yourself and others. You choose to live out God's will daily so that He gets the ultimate victory. You realize now that you can no longer feed your fleshly desires, such as partaking in activities and things that do not line up with the Word (giving up your life), to pursue after the things of Christ (gaining life).

Prayer: Dear Lord, I Thank You for Your Word that teaches me Your ways. My prayer Lord is that I am careful to deny myself and follow Your will so that I may gain. My desire is to glorify You in all that I say and do!

8. Encouragement:

Philippians 4:13 (NKJV) - I can do all things through Christ who strengthens me.

**The key here is to remember that nothing is too hard for Christ, and if you seek him first in all things you can do it. Not in our strength but rely on His strength to get us through it. **

Prayer: Father God, allow Your strength to work in me and help me to realize that You are my strength.

9. Faith:

Hebrews 11:1 (NIV) - Now faith is confidence in what we hope for and assurance about what we do not see.

Faith may seem different to understand because we can't see it. However, we test faith every day, for example, we sit in a chair and practice faith that it will hold us up when we sit in it. We also practice faith when we step outside and we don't see the wind but we can feel it. That same faith we have in those things is the same faith we are to utilize when it comes to Christ and letting Him lead you through life and believing He knows best.

Prayer: Lord allow me to exercise my Faith in you daily. Give me the strength and ability to give you my life to rule over because I know that you are my Father and you know what is best for me.

10. Forgiveness:

Ephesians 4:32 (NIV) -Be kind and compassionate to one another, forgiving each other, just as in Christ God forgave you."

**Holding on to forgiveness causes a heavy weight for you to carry. It causes unnecessary stress which can lead to health issues. Our job is to love and forgive all just as we would expect from someone whom we have wronged. Think about it, if Christ can forgive those who persecuted and tortured him, then who are we to not do the same. **

11. Obedience:

1 Peter 1:14 (NIV) - As obedient children, do not conform to the evil desires you had when you lived in ignorance.

**This verse is urging you to stay the course with God and not go back to your old ways that lead to destruction. Remember why it is that you decided to make a change and continue toward the goal. **

Prayer: Lord God please be my eyes, my thoughts, my steps so that I am very careful to not revert back to my old self that is not any good for me. But I will continue the path with you and bring others along the way.

12. Reconciliation:

II Corinthians 5:18-19 (NIV) - All this is from God, who reconciled us to Himself through Christ and gave us the ministry of reconciliation: that God was reconciling the world to himself in Christ, not counting people's sins against them. And He has committed to us the message of reconciliation.

**Reconcile can mean "compatible" or "restore" with each other. Wow, compatible, re-read the verse and think of being compatible to Christ and in the second verse God Restoring the world. God is about relationships, compatible and restoring are two components of just that. **

Prayer: Thank you Lord, for thinking that much of me that You want to have a relationship someone like me. Despite the wrong that I have done toward You, You still have not count me out, and for this I give Thanks!

13. Suffering:

James 1:12 (NIV) - Blessed is the one who perseveres under trial because, having stood the test, that person will receive the crown of life that the Lord has promised to those who love Him.

**When you are going through test and trials here on earth, it is important that we stand firm on God's Truth so that we will pass and bring Glory to His name. Not all rewards are given here on earth, remember you are also storing up treasures in heaven. **

Prayer: Help me, Lord, to persevere under pressure for Your name's sake, but I also ask for Your forgiveness for the times that I fail. For when I fail, help me to realize that I have turned from You and to quickly return.

14. Temptation:

James 1:13-15 (NIV)

When tempted, no one should say, "God is tempting me." For God cannot be tempted by evil, nor does He tempt anyone, but each person is tempted when they are dragged away by their own evil desire and enticed. Then, after desire has conceived, it gives birth to sin, and sin, when it is full-grown, gives birth to death.

**Temptation is everywhere! You have to be wise enough to know what you can handle and what you cannot. We are to be very careful not to put ourselves in situations that cause us to sin. When we find ourselves in sin, we are to quickly flee so that sin does not become a normal thing in our life, which then leads to spiritual death (separation from God)! **

Prayer: Father God my prayer is to remove people and things in our life that cause us to sin and help us Lord God not to be a stumbling block to others as well!

15. Trust:

Psalms 28:7 (NIV) - The Lord is my strength and my shield, my heart trusts in Him, and He helps me. My heart leaps for joy, and with my song I praise Him.

**Can you see how your life would be if you were to fully put your Trust in Christ? This is a daily practice for all, but think about it. Why not Trust the one who made the universe and made you, after all, your creator knows you better than you know yourself. So why not trust Him?

Prayer: Father, I thank you for all you have done for me! As I sit back and look over my life at all you have brought me through, my heart is full of joy! So forgive me for the times that I fail in trusting you wholeheartedly!

16. Wisdom:

Proverbs 11:12 (NIV) - When pride comes, then comes disgrace, but with humility comes wisdom.

**To have wisdom you have to be humble. Humble means to not be boastful or prideful. You don't come off as a person being better than others because you may have more of something than another. However, pride is a whole different thing; pride will cause you to be alone. It will make you boastful and feel as though you are superior to others. Sometimes it can get so bad that you will think you are better than God. Humble people are always willing to learn, which in return, gains wisdom. Pride will make you unteachable, which leads to destruction. **

Prayer: Father God allow me to not get so beside myself in this life that I become unteachable and drift away from you. I want to always rely on your guidance and teachings.

17. Worrying:

Matthew 6:25-28, 34 (NIV)
Therefore, I tell you, do not worry about your life, what you will eat or drink; or about your body, what you will wear. Is not life more than your

clothes. Look at the birds of the air; they do not sow or reap or store away in barns, and yet your heavenly Father feeds them. Are you not much more valuable than they? Can any one of you by worrying add a single hour to your life? And why do you worry about clothes? See how the flowers of the field grow. They do not labor or spin. Therefore, do not worry about tomorrow, for tomorrow will worry about itself. Each day has enough troubles of its own.

**As you can see from the verses above, the key takeaway is to not worry: God provides all and takes care of all his creation. So, ask for what you need for today, and let tomorrow worry about itself. Worrying only means that we do not Trust and that, my dear friend, is not from God. **

Prayer: Lord God if I say I trust You let me truly depend on You. So I am not to worry about anything, however, when worrying creeps up, let me give You praise through it!

18. Joy:

I Peter 1:8-9 (NIV) Though you have not seen Him, you Love Him, even though you do not see Him now, you believe in Him and are filled with an inexpressible and glorious joy, for you are receiving the end result of your faith, the salvation of your souls.

**We get great joy in knowing Christ and loving Him even though we cannot physically see Him. This goes back to practicing Faith. The even greater joy is knowing that we have salvation in Him forever! **

Prayer: Lord what pleasure I have in learning of you and drawing close to You. I have an ever greater love knowing Christ died to save my soul!

19. Hope:

Isaiah 40:31 (NIV) -But those who hope in the Lord will renew their strength. They will soar on wings like eagles, they will run and not grow weary, and they will walk and not be faint.

**Hope is referring to Trust in this scripture, so when we find ourselves getting tired during this Christian journey. We can turn to God and trust that He will renew our strength to continue the race. **

Prayer: Lord, I pray that my strength and hope be renewed in you daily so that I may finish the race!

20. Love:

John 3:16 (KJV) - For God so loved the world that He gave His only begotten son, that whosoever believe in Him shall not perish but have everlasting life.

** This is the most sacrificial act of love that anyone can do. This is how much God loves you and me. This act of unconditional love is what gives you the opportunity to everlasting life. Don't let the opportunity to become a child of the most high God pass you by. **

Prayer: Thank you God for sending Your son to save humanity. Let us not take for granted Your act of love for us all. I pray that we will not miss out on the opportunity to become a child of Yours eternally. We love You and adore You.
In Jesus' name,
Amen

Reflection

About the Author

LaToya Sneed was born in Louisville, KY and later raised by her grandparents in New Albany, IN. She loves attending church with her family and participating in any outreach opportunities that allows her to engage with the community around her. This is where her passion for Christ shows up the most!

One of her goals is to reach as many young teens and share with them the precious love of Christ.

She has 5 young men that God has allowed her the opportunity to watch over: Elijah (17), Zion (12), Bryan (10), George (6) and Avrie (2).

Last, but surely not least, the Love of my life, Marquis, whom I Truly adore, appreciate and enjoy walking this Christian journey together!

To connect with LaToya Sneed, email her at latoyasneed31@yahoo.com or follow her on social media at:

Facebook @latoya.sneed
Instagram @latoyasneed31

www.ingramcontent.com/pod-product-compliance
Lightning Source LLC
Chambersburg PA
CBHW051706090426
42736CB00013B/2571